Simple Small Business

77 Free and Low Cost Ways Proven To Attract New Customers, In Any Economic Climate

Includes 3 Bonus Sections:

7 Marketing Mistakes That Destroy Business Profits

4 Powerful Strategies Guaranteed To Grow Any Business

How to Quickly & Profitably Grow Any Business With Little Or No Additional Money Or Risk

by Michael John Alos

Published by

Growth Publications, LLC
www.GrowthPublications.com

Printed in the United States of America

This publication is designed to provide accurate and authoritative information with regard to the subject matter covered. It is sold with the understanding that the publisher is not engaged in rendering legal, accounting, or other professional advice. If legal advice or other expert assistance is required, the services of a competent professional person should be sought.

- From a *Declaration of Principles* jointly adopted by a Committee of the American Bar Association and a Committee of Publishers and Associations.

This book is available at quantity discounts for bulk purchases. For information, visit www.CustomerAttractionBook.com

ISBN-10: 0615583660
ISBN-13: 978-0-615-58366-2

Table of Contents

How To Use This Book

Every Customer Attractor in this book has been selected to help you attract a steady stream of new customers.

Don't try to implement all 77 Customer Attractors at once. Some might be a good fit for your business now and others might work better for you at a later time. Read through this book in its' entirety first. Then select only those Customer Attractors that can really make a difference in your business immediately.

Involve your staff in selecting and implementing each Customer Attractors and don't forget to give them credit for their success.

Invest in additional copies of this book and distribute them among your staff. Get everyone involved in selecting and recommending the various Customer Attractors.

Revisit this book every 90 days. As your business grows, you'll find that some Customer Attractors work better now than they did previously.

Remember, all the ideas in this book have been proven in businesses across the United States and around the world. They have worked for others and will work for you!

If at anytime you have any questions or need help implementing any of the strategies outlined in this book, you may contact me at www.MichaelAlos.com.

Customer Attractor #1
Make Marketing Your Business
<u>THE</u> Top Priority

Marketing is the only thing that drives your business. Unfortunately, quite a few businesses get this wrong. Instead they focus on the creation of their product, not the marketing of their product.

Marketing is what attracts new prospects, prospects become customers. Marketing must be an essential part of every business and focused on daily. When you need to increase your business profits, focus on increasing your marketing.

If you're not already, set aside a predetermined amount of time each day to market your business. Make this time a commitment, put it into your daily schedule and don't let anything interrupt you during your marketing time.

It's during your marketing time when you'll development new advertisements and new marketing campaigns. You'll also research what methods your competition is using to grow their businesses.

Customer Attractor #2
Low-Cost or Introductory Packages

A great strategy for easing your prospects into their buying decision is by offering a low-cost or an introductory package of your product or service.

One industry that I commonly do quite a bit of consulting work is the martial arts industry. Introduction offers are used quite often in this industry to attract new students to a martial arts school.

The specific offer varies from school to school, depending on how much the school owner wants to spend to acquire a new student but usually an introductory offer include the following:

- The prospective student can train at the school for 30 days free

- The prospective student gets a free training uniform

- Various other training equipment and gear

- Possibly a gift certificate valid for a few private training sessions if they become a student

The average cost of the entire introductory package can range from $150 to $500 depending on what is included.

The school owner can afford to give away this sort of package because typical a new student signs a one or two year committal contract. So the owner will not only recoup the cost of the introductory package but he will also have a new student paying monthly over the next 12 or 24 months.

Customer Attractor #3
Tell Them What To Do Next

How you end your sales presentations or sales letters are crucial to gaining new customers. The one important thing you must do is to direct your prospect to take some sort of action.

The action you want them to may be one of the following if you're writing them a sales letter:

- Pick up the phone and order now

- Fill in the order coupon and mail it in the return envelop

- Visit our web site at www.YourSite.com and click the Order link

- Come into our store today

You never want your prospect to have to think about what action they should take next. Whenever possible, take your prospect by the hand and lead them through each step of your sales process.

If you don't lead them through your sales process, you're leaving your profits in the hands of their buying process.

Do you want your prospects controlling your sales?

Customer Attractor #4
Get Rid of the Attitudes

You're doing everything right in your business. You have a great product, you have great advertising but your still not getting all the new customers you need.

Your staff might be the reason why. Have you ever had the experience of walking into a store knowing exactly what you want and having your wallet in your hand only to walk out empty handed?

People work had for their money and the last thing they want is someone being rude when they are trying to make a purchase. I can't tell you the number of times I've been ready to buy and all they had to do is pull the item out from behind the counter and ring me up, but I walked out empty handed.

Each staff member that deals with your prospects and customers is a crucial part of your marketing department. They might not be directly selling or developing advertising campaigns but they are shaping the perception of your business in the minds of each and every person that walks in.

Do you know how you're employees are treating your customers? If not, maybe it's time for you play customer. You can hire a mystery shopper firm to play customer for you or you can simply pick up the phone and call a random sample of customers and ask them about how the buying experience was for them.

Customer Attractor #5
Let Your Employees Lead
You To New Customers

The idea of social networking has created a new avenue for businesses to find hot new prospects. The premise behind social networking is that if you and I are friends, then you can become friends with my friends. Automatically widening each other's circle of influence.

Don't underestimate the circle of influence of your employees. Just because they work for you, doesn't mean that they don't know someone, or know someone who knows someone, who might be interested in doing business with you.

Throughout all my years as a consultant, I've only come across one business that was actively looking into their employee's social network for new prospects.

Another thing to remember is that the friends and family of your employees also have lives and they also have jobs. So just because an employee's friend might not need your product or service, do they work for a company that could benefit from what your business offers? Then you can use that relationship (or network) to get the door opened for your sales staff.

Customer Attractor #6
Stop Treating Everyone The Same

A critical mistake that many businesses make, even the large corporate ones, it they use "one size fits all" marketing when offering their products or services to different market segments. This strategy typically results in very low sales conversions.

The requirements of each market segment may vary considerably thus so should your marketing strategy, marketing message and the media you use to reach each market segment.

To begin, you should clearly define the different market segments that you're targeting. Then look at each segment and look for similarities and differences between the two. Do they use different terms? Do they have different needs?

Once you have a better understanding of each segment, prepare a custom and tailored marketing message for each segment.

Customer Attractor #7
Reduce the Fear Factor

Ever buy a used car? I dislike buying a used cars and 15 years ago I vowed never to buy a used car again.

Why do I dislike buying a used car so much? Because the used car industry is filled with shady sellers and crooks. They sell a car "as is" and once you drive it off the car lot, if anything goes wrong it's your problem.

Sure there are lemon laws and laws specifically regarding these types of business practices but who wants to go through all those headaches and paperwork.

What if a salesman told me to take the car home for a week, drive it, try it out, take it to another mechanic and get a second opinion? Do you think that would alleviate some of the fear I have about buying a used car?

You bet it would!

In the world of marketing, we call this "risk reversal". Risk reversal is nothing more than taking the risk away from your prospect and putting all the risk on your shoulders.

When someone is on the fence about making a purchase it's usually because they want to make sure they're not getting taken advantage of, that they are getting the best deal. Everyone hates to make a purchase today and then see it advertised for less at another store tomorrow. We feel like we were taken advantage of.

A great way to get any prospect to buy from you instead of your competition is to reverse the risk. You could reverse the risk by:

- Offering a "no questions asked 100% money back guarantee"
- "Try it before you buy" type of program
- Take it home today and not charge for 30 days

The specific risk reversal strategy you use deeps on your business. Just remember aim of using a risk reversal is to take the risk of making a purchase away from your prospect.

Customer Attractor #8
Open Your Mouth

Even though this strategy is simple, I'm going to guess only 20% of the people who read this book will do it.

Simply make sure your friends, family and vendors know exactly what you do in your business and ask them to keep you in mind if they meet someone who is looking for what you offer.

Let your friends know that you're looking for new customers and that you would appreciate their help.

People are very shy when it comes to asking for something. Don't be shy, they're your friends who'll be looking out for your best interest.

Customer Attractor #9
Recycling Dollars

I call this strategy my Golden Rule. I do my best to abide by this rule whenever I can.

My Golden Rule is called Recycling Dollars.

It's really simple to understand. If I do business with you, I expect you to do business with me when you need the services I offer.

So if my dentist needs marketing advice, I expect him to give me a call. As long as I offer what he needs and can help him, I expect him to hire me.

Here's how the actual recycling works, I pay him $100 for my dental work. Now he buys one of marketing courses for $97. In essence, he has paid me back the $100 I gave him.

Now it's not an exact science but I hope you get the point I'm attempting to make.

Recycling also sets the scene for bartering services later down the road.

Customer Attractor #10
Barter Your Services

There are times when money might be an issue for a prospect. They simply might not have the money necessary to compensate you for your product or service.

Money is not the only way to get paid. You can also barter your product for a product or service that they offer of equal value. Barter is basically trading your item, for an item of theirs.

With barter you can get very creative. Maybe instead of trading product for product, you ask your barter partner to introduce you to the CEO of one of their customers for a potential sale.

Here are a few simple examples of barter:

- A dentist who needs the services of a plumber can barter his dental services for the plumber's services.

- A graphic designer in need of chiropractic services could better a new logo and letterhead design for a few chiropractic sessions.

- A new carpet store in need of office furniture could barter re-carpet the showroom of a furniture store for much needed office furniture.

There are many benefits of barter and many ways to set up a barter arrangement. If you're interested in using barter as a profit center for your business, contact my office for a copy of my barter course at www.MichaelAlos.com.

Customer Attractor #11
Get On The Phone

If you're in business I'll bet you any amount of money that you have a phone. Each month you're paying that phone bill whether you make one call or thousand calls.

It costs you virtually nothing, other than time, to pick up the phone and dial the phone number of people who are a great fit for the product or service you offer.

If you provide a product to businesses, simply get on the Internet and go to your favorite search engine and search for websites of businesses that fit the profile of your ideal customer. Visit their site, click on their contact link, get their phone number and give them a call.

Note: Please be aware of the telemarketing laws for your state before implementing this strategy.

Customer Attractor #12
Community Bulletin Boards

This is a great free strategy if you provide a service at the local level. I've seen a few plumbers and contractors have great success with this.

Each community has businesses that have bulletin boards where people can post lost dog signs along with their business cards. Just create an ad for your business and post them on each bulletin board.

Places where you'll commonly find community bulletin boards are:

- Book stores
- Coffee shops
- Convenience stores
- Hardware stores
- Post offices
- Local banks

If you don't have the time or the energy to post them on each board yourself, you can hire a local high school kid to go around and post them for you.

Customer Attractor #13
Give Them A Bonus

A well-known secret in the mail order industry is the use of bonuses. It's been proven that people will actually buy the main product just to get their hands on the bonus that's being offered.

A great place to spot bonuses at work is during those sixty-second television commercials. The main product sold during the commercial is a garden tool and if you call and order the garden tool in the next 30 minutes, they'll include two additional (but different) garden tools free.

The bonus in the above example is the two additional garden tools.

You're not limited to what you offer as a bonus as long as you keep two things in mind:

1. The bonus must be related or complimentary to the main product your customer is buying

2. The bonus must have a high perceived value

Bonuses can be used by any business. A restaurant can use a dessert as a bonus. A pizza shop can give away a 2-liter of soda with every order. A hardware store can offer a set or paint brushes with ever 10 gallons of paint that you order.

As a purchaser of this book, you are entitled to free bonus gifts valued at $47. To grab your free bonus gifts, visit www.CustomerAttractionBook.com/free

---

Customer Attractor #14
Guarantees Guarantee Sales

A great way to attract new customers is to stand behind your product or service by offering a guarantee. In most cases, the stronger the guarantee, the more new customers you'll attract and the more sales you'll close.

Guarantees work because your prospect feels assured that what you offer will work as promised or if they have any problems with it, you'll stand behind your workmanship.

Determining what guarantee works best for your business will take some testing. If you have a product that you don't feel comfortable offering a guarantee on, then you should think twice about selling it.

In my own business, I offer 100% Money Back Guarantees on just about every marketing course I sell. Sure a few people take advantage of this type of guarantee by buying the course, making a photocopy and then returning it for a full-refund.

But there will always be a few bad apples. The number of bad apples who have taken advantage of my guarantee are few. Besides, these bad apples go onto my "bad apple list" and I reserve the right never to do business with them again.

Customer Attractor #15
Make The Benefits Stand Out

People are busier today than ever before. Our lives are full of distractions. So wouldn't it make sense to make it easier for your prospect to discover the benefits of your product or service?

Your prospects don't want to spend time reading a lengthy brochure where all the benefits of your product are hidden in wordy paragraphs.

Make it easy for them by using 'bullets' to make the benefits of your products stand out.

What exactly is a bullet? A bullet is a single line statement that states a benefit of your product or service.

Here are a few examples of bullets that I use to describe my Business Coaching program:

- Create systems that will have your business running on autopilot.

- Build a customer base that generates 3 to 5 times the current revenue it's amazing that less than 0.01% of businesses are using this technique!

- Get anywhere from 2 - 7 times the amount of referrals from your current customer that you're getting now and your customers will be lining up to give you these referrals!

- Get started marketing your business with low budget (or no budget) techniques even if you don't have a huge marketing budget, you can still get the results of the "big boys"

- Tap your in-house customer list to generate more profits in the next 30 days than you ever thought possible if you are not consistently marketing to your customer list, you're walking away from a virtual goldmine

- Revive past customers like never before (if a good amount of clients have left your business, don't worry - there are techniques to bring them back!)

Bullets make reading quicker and the reader doesn't feel overwhelmed with information. Each bullet discusses a benefit of becoming a member in my coaching program and leaves the reading interested in learning more.

Take a look at your current marketing and advertising materials and see where you can use bullets.

If you would like to learn more about my business coaching program visit www.MichaelAlos.com.

Customer Attractor #16
Sell The Benefits Not The Features

This is a very common mistake that businesses make in their advertising and marketing efforts. By changing all your marketing materials to list the benefits of your product, you'll start to notice a tremendous increase in new business.

A feature is just that, it's a feature of your product. If I were to use a car as an example, the following would be features:

- 4 door

- 17-inch polished aluminum wheels

- Front and rear passenger air bags

- Cup holders

- AM/FM stereo with CD player and MP3 playback

Those are features of a car. Not very exciting and it doesn't make me want to rush out and buy this car.

If I was a father of two children and I was looking for a car, let's see if this next set of bullets would get my attention:

- The two rear doors are automatic sliding doors that open from a touch of a button on the easy to carry combination key chain and door remote.

- The tires are mounted on high quality aircraft aluminum that will handle the bumps and potholes on the toughest city highways. Not only are they tough but the aluminum is polished to a shine that will make your neighbors envious.

- Accidents happen, but know can sleep well at night knowing your wife and children are surrounded by rapid deploying air bags.

- Hate your morning commute to the office? Now you'll look forward to it. The car comes with four no-spill cups holders that keep your latte secure and warm. While you enjoy all the tunes on your MP3 playlist using the quick-connect MP3 plugin.

Now those are some benefits!

The features merely pointed out a feature of the car. The benefits described, appealing to my emotions, how those features would actually benefit me.

Features tell, Benefits sell!

Customer Attractor #17
Make It Easy For Your
Prospects To Contact You

As a consumer, this has to be my biggest pet peeve. I'm interested in buying a product and I visit the company's web site but I have a question. I want an answer to this question before I place my order.

So naturally I want to call or email the company. In many cases, companies make it very difficult to find their contact information on their web site.

This may be intentional or this may be unintentional. Maybe they had they web site designed by a creative advertising firm that designed a fancy site without keeping the customer in mind.

Like it or not, prospects will have questions. Some prospects may just want to call and talk to a living, breathing human being before they place an order.

On your web site and promotional materials, make your contact information easy to find. Include a link to your company's contact information on every page. If you have a retail location, then include easy-to-follow directions on your website.

Customer Attractor #18
Direct Mail Gives You A Big Bang At Low Cost

Direct mail is either loved or hated as a method of getting new customers. Those who love it, know exactly how to profitably use it. Those who hate direct mail are doing it wrong.

Direct mail is nothing more than putting your marketing message on paper and letting the postal service deliver it to your prospects for you.

Typically a direct mail campaign consists of a sales letter, an envelope and a response mechanism. The sales letter is a letter that explains that benefits of the product you're offering and how they can order it.

The response mechanism can be an order form that your prospect completes and faxes back to you. And of course the envelope is just an envelope to send your letter in.

One benefit to using direct mail is the availability of mailing lists. There are businesses that specialize in compiling and renting lists of every type of consumer and business imaginable and make them available for rental.

Once you rent the list, you have the right to mail your marketing message to that list. If your message and offer are matched correctly with the list, you'll get orders for your product.

Say your company does most of its' selling by telephone. How many sales could one sales person make in one hour? Well, it depends on how long it takes to deliver the sales pitch and how many questions the prospect has. For discussion sake, let's assume you can make one sale every sixty minutes.

If I took that exact same script that your telephone sales person is using on the phone and put it into a letter and then mailed that letter to 1,000 people on a targeted mailing list, how many sales might I be able to make in an hour?

What If I sent my sales letter to 2,000? How about 10,000 people on a targeted mailing list?

That's a main benefit of direct mail. I can target thousands of people by using a letter that's delivered by the postal service.

There's much more to direct mail and many ways to create a sales letter that will appeal to your prospects emotions and get them eager to buy. This brief explanation doesn't do it the justice it deserves. If you want to seriously use to direct mail to grow your business, contact my office and inquire about one of my many direct mail courses.

Customer Attractor #19
Door To Door Sales Isn't Dead

Do you have a product or service that lends itself to door-to-door sales? If your product can be demonstrated in the home then door to door selling might be a great way to reach customers.

The following lend themselves perfectly for door-to-door selling:

- Books
- Small appliances
- Cookware and utensils
- Toys
- Health products
- Jewelry
- Clothing

And the list goes on.

Why not start canvasing your neighborhood today and introduce yourself to your neighbors and tell them what you do and the benefits of the products you sell.

Customer Attractor #20
Infomercials Can Get You
Millions Of New Customers

On a national level this might not be the most low cost method available but on a local level infomercials might be a great fit for your product.

An infomercial is nothing more than a thirty-minute television show that's created to sell your product. The show is actually a sales presentation that's put together in such a way to make it appear to be a real television program about your product or service.

Airtime for a infomercial can be quite expense but if you're interested in only airing your infomercial to your local television market, you'll be surprised on how affordable it can be.

Customer Attractor #21
Pay People To Try Your Product

Car manufacturers have been paying people to take test-drives for years. Sometimes it's in the form of cash and other times in the form of gift certificates.

If you're confident people will love your product once they try it, give them $50 or a $50 gift certificate to come in and try your product out.

Another method you could use is to give any a $50 credit towards purchase if they come in this weekend and try your product.

Customer Attractor #22
Bribe Your Customers To
Do Business With You

Sure a bribe might be a little unethical but how about we call it giving your prospects a reason to stop into your business.

Here are a few examples:

- A coffee shop that also serves sandwiches and food might offer free coffee from noon to 1:00 pm to anyone who comes in. Since it's lunchtime and people are coming in for coffee, they'll be more inclined to grab a sandwich.

- A hardware store could offer a weekly barbecue and free food to attract contractors to come into their store.

- A video store could easily offer "rent one, get one rental free" day each week.

A bribe is nothing more than giving your prospect a little extra value to make a purchase from you. The bribe will depend on what product you sell but is not limited to businesses that sell tangible products.

What extra incentives could you use to create more sales from your prospects?

_____

_____

_____

_____

_____

Customer Attractor #23
Article Marketing

Writing articles is a great way to give your prospects a glimpse into your knowledge and position yourself as an expert in your respective field. What most businesses don't realize is that articles can be a great source of new customers.

If you're saying that you could never write and article, you're wrong. If you know enough about a topic to have a conversation with someone on that topic, then you can write an article on that topic.

I suggest two ways for you to start writing articles. The first is to sit in front of your computer, open up your word processing program and begin to outline your thoughts on a single topic. Once you have the outline complete, go back and fill in outline with supporting information.

If you're someone who types slow or hates to type, don't worry, I have a solution. With this second method, you still need an outline to organize your thoughts but this time instead of typing, grab a digital voice recorder or a microcassette recorder and talk your article into the recorder. Then through your local Yellow Pages or Craigslist.org, find someone to transcribe your audio into a document.

Once you have your article you can submit your article to publishers of trade journals or other print media that your prospects might read.

Another great source of new customers comes by submitting your articles to article directories on the Internet. These are directories then take your articles and distribute them to other web sites in their network. Article directories work to get your articles all over the Internet.

Having your article and name all over the Internet makes it easier for your potential prospects to find you online.

Customer Attractor #24
Pay-Per-Click Internet Marketing

You might be asking…"doesn't pay-per-click marketing cost a lot of money?" The answer to that question is both yes and no.

Pay-per-click marketing is when you advertise on a search engine and the search engine charges you each time someone clicks on your ad.

Google has the Internet's most well known pay-per-click program that is called Adwords. When you create an Adwords marketing campaign, you place small ads on the screen when someone uses Google to search for something.

With pay-per-click marketing, you place bids on keywords. Keywords are the words that people type into a search engine and the search engine displays the results that are the best match for that keyword. Google let's their advertisers bid on those keywords.

The bid amount for some keywords can be a few cents while for other keywords it can be tens-of-dollars. The great news is that those keywords that cost tens-of-dollars are so generic that the people that are typing them into Google are just looking for information, they are not necessarily ready to buy.

You can take advantage of pay-per-click by finding those keywords that are very specific to what you sell. For example if you were cellular phone store instead of bidding on "Motorola cell phone" you would choose a more specific keyword like "Motorola MOTO Q 9c".

Someone who is searching for a very specific model is more likely to buy than the person typing in generic keywords. This means that the probability of making a sale when someone clicks on your pay-per-click ad is greater. Thus you're spending your pay-per-click budget in a more efficient manner.

Customer Attractor #25
Offer You Product Or Service As Premiums To Other Business

Sometimes all it takes is getting a customer in the door once and because of your knock'em dead service, you know have that customer for life.

By teaming up with other businesses may be just what you need to get new customers in the door. Your product or service, when added to another company' own product or service, can really create one heck of a package.

Here are a few examples:

- A restaurant could offer $100 gift certificates to a few real estate agents in the area to give to every new home buyer.

- A dentist could give a cosmetic surgeon a voucher valid for free teeth whitening session.

- A home painter could give a real estate agent voucher valid for one room painted free when they get three rooms painted if they purchase a home from the agent.

Take this book for example, if your customers are small and medium size businesses, this book would make a great gift to give to you customer's CEO, sales team or marketing department.

By you teaming up with another business and giving them an item to give to their customers, your business is getting exposure and the value of what they offer has a higher perceived value.

Customer Attractor #26
Attend Your Local Flea Markets
And Swap Meets

During the summer there are flea markets everywhere. A flea market or swap meet is a place where vendors come to sell or trade their goods.

To exhibit your goods at a flea market you're usually charged a table fee. The fee can be anywhere from a few dollars to a few hundred of dollars depending on the size of the flea market.

People go to flea markets looking for a deal. So why not give them one.

A house painter could rent a table at the flea market and bring all the before and after photos of the houses he painted. He should also create an offer specifically for people at the flea market.

A message therapist could rent a table and bring his message table and give people free five-minute messages. He could also have a small television playing a DVD of testimonials of happy patients and offer special discounts specifically the flea market attendees.

This might take a little change in mindset but there's nothing wrong with advertising at a flea market. You should be thanking the flea market promoter because he has rounded-up a bunch of potential customers for you and put them all in one place.

Customer Attractor #27
Trade Shows Are Where The Gold Is

Trade shows can be a great source of new customers for any business in two ways:

First, of course, you can become an exhibitor at the show by renting floor space and setting up a booth. If your display materials that attract attention and are of interest to passer-bys, visitors will stop by your booth and inquire about your product or services.

Let's look at a second way trade shows can be a great source of prospects.

Industry trade shows are usually a very big deal. The happen once or twice and year and every business in that industry wants to be there.

Have you ever actually stopped to think about who attends a trade show?

Of course you get staff members and rank-and-file employees but you also get the executive management of businesses in that industry.

This becomes quite useful if you're a sales person who has been trying get an appointment with a certain CEO for some time. A great place to casually bumped into that CEO would be his or her industry's trade show.

Just make sure you have your pitch and presentation down. You may only get a few seconds of that CEO's time.

Customer Attractor #28
Start An Electronic Newsletter

Wouldn't life be great if every time someone visited your website they bought something? It's one thing if someone leaves without buying, it's a whole another thing if they leave and you don't even know who they are.

There's a great asset in knowing who's visiting your website. There can be many reasons why someone visits your site and doesn't buy. The good news is that if someone did visit , it's likely they're interested in what you're selling.

By capturing the information of every person who visits your site, you start to build a list of prospective customers whom you can continue to follow up with and continue to build a relationship with.

The most popular methods of capturing visitor information is by offering something of value. They need to "opt-in" or request this free item of value. In most cases, this item of value is in the form of:

- Whitepapers

- Special reports

- eBooks (books delivered typically in PDF format)

- Electronic newsletters (ezines)

The information that you collect on your prospect varies, but at minimum, collect at least first name and email address. Once the visitor enters this information, they're given access to free report.

Get Your Free Copy of My Small Business Marketing eCourse.

✔ YES! Grant me access to the eCrouse. I'll just type in my name and email, then click the Subscribe button.

Your Name:
Your Email:

Subscribe

🔒 Your privacy is protected.

To the right is an example of an ezine opt-in form from a website. In this example, we are collecting the first name and email address of the visitors to my site. Once the click the "Subscribe" button, they'll receive a weekly electronic newsletter (ezine) delivered to the email address they entered in the box.

Each week in my ezine, I deliver just a taste of the some of the same advice that my clients pay my thousands of dollars for.

If you're not already receiving my "Acquire, Maximize, Retain eCourse", head over to www.MichaelAlos.com to sign up.

Customer Attractor #29
Affiliate Internet Marketing

Wouldn't be great to have an army of people selling your products or services at no expense to you until they make a sale?

The Internet has made this a reality. You can quickly and easily setup an affiliate program and recruit others to sell any product you offer.

An affiliate program is basically this, you give your affiliates a special link to your website or a specific product on your website. In return, your affiliates advertise this special link. The people that advertise your special link are called affiliates.

When someone clicks on this special link, a tracking code is placed on the person's computer. The tracking is unnoticeable to the visitor.

This tracking code is used to monitor whether visitors sent by this special link actually makes a purchase. Then and only then if the visitor makes a purchase do you pay your affiliate.

How you pay your affiliates vary but usually they are paid affiliate commissions for any sales in the past 30 days.

An affiliate program is a win-win for you and your affiliate partners because:

- You get "no-risk" advertising. In most cases, you wouldn't pay your affiliates unless they make a sale.

- Your affiliate gets the opportunity to earn extra income without the hassle of producing a product and all the overhead business.

There's not many things that are more profitable for a business than having someone else pay to market their product or service.

Customer Attractor #30
Blog To Attract New Customers

Blogging is a great way to attract new customers to your business. Blogging has two great advantages over every other forms of Internet marketing:

1. Blogging doesn't cost anything other than time.

2. Search engines love blogs and they get ranked quickly.

If you don't know how to setup a blog on your business' website, there are plenty of free blogging services available. Google offers a free blogging service at www.Blogger.com. All you need is an email address to get started.

When you blog, you simply write small stories, reviews, tips and tricks, educational information, etc. all related to the product or service you offer. If the readers of your blog find your "content" beneficial, or entertaining, they'll frequent your blog often to stay abreast of your writings.

Customer Attractor #31
Leave Your Card Everywhere You Go

I don't think I've ever met someone in business that doesn't have a business card. In fact, a business card is typically the first thing anyone going into business gets – even before they come up with a marketing plan.

Business cards are very inexpensive nowadays. They typically cost a few pennies each depending on how fancy you get and you can get them by the thousands. Using the Internet to do a quick search, you can get 5,000 cards for roughly $150 with printing on both sides. That's pretty darn cheap!

Because cards are so inexpensive, you should be giving them out to everyone you meet. Just think of all the people you meet or bump into on a regular basis:

- Grocery clerks
- Post office workers
- Family members
- Friends
- Salesmen
- Doctors
- Dentists

Not only should you be giving your card out to everyone you meet or bump into, but you might also want to consider leaving a card behind wherever you visit a business.

If you eat at a restaurant, leave your card on the table when you leave.

Customer Attractor #32
Give Some To Charity

Find a charity your target audience would likely support. Explain in your advertising or to everyone that visits your store that a percentage of the profits of each sale go to that specific charity.

To take it a step further, for each person that makes a purchase send them a thank you card letting them know that you appreciate their support and so does the charity. This will definitely remind them they did the right thing and encourage the behavior of giving.

You could also run a press release and let the public know about your charity promotion and encourage everyone to stop by and make a purchase.

Customer Attractor #33
Tie Into the Holidays

Use holidays as a reason to get free publicity. Write a press release or article about your product or service and how it ties into the current holiday. It'll have a higher chance of being published or picked up as a news a story.

For example, your title could be, "10 ways to not overeat during Thanksgiving weekend" Another example, "How to get your husband to buy you that something special for Valentine's Day".

Your local television stations love stories like this. My local stations love things with an edge that tie into any current event or holiday.

Customer Attractor #34
Use Free Information To
Attract New Customers

When you forget about trying to make a sale and start providing useful information, you position yourself as more knowledgeable, experienced, skilled and more service-oriented than any of your competitors.

With the development of new technologies, information can be produced very inexpensively and offered in a variety of formats and increase the perceived value of the information.

Simply by offering useable advice, your prospects will trust you and be more likely to give you their business. This trust factor will eliminate your prospects resistance to price, allowing you to charge more for your product or service.

You can package and deliver the information in a wide range of formats; Books, Cassettes, CD-ROMs, DVDs, Articles, White Papers and/or Special Reports.

All of the above can very effective ways to distribute your free information and communicate you as the "go to person" in your industry.

Since the free information that you're distributing just isn't promotional material about your products, this information tends to receive greater acceptance in the marketplace while helping to sell you and your company as the industry leaders.

Keep your free information educational and relevant to what your prospects want or can benefit from. Your goal should be to showcase your specific knowledge, experience and skills. In doing this, you'll raise your prospect's awareness and perception of what your offer beyond your products and services.

Customer Attractor #35
Offer a Free Newsletter Subscription

Not only is this a great strategy to nurture current customers but also it's very effective for attracting new customers. Either way, you'll find that publishing a newsletter certainty will have far reaching results.

Newsletters are a great Customer Attractor because they are perceived to be informative, contain useable ideas and product news. By delivering value in your newsletter, your prospects can look forward to each value packed issue.

How often you publish your newsletter is really up to you. At minimum you should aim to publish once per month. Twelve touches to each prospect is a minimum, I would recommend that you publish twice a month.

A great little strategy is to publish case studies in each issue. A case study is basically just social proof that your product or service delivers as promised. As your prospects are exposed to each issue, they'll read stories of the success your current customers are having by doing business with you and start to feel that they are missing out on success.

If you do business in multiple niches, considering making a newsletter template. Each template contains 80% of the same information except the case studies are different for each niche.

Use the success stories of customers you have in that niche. So if you sell to chiropractors and dentists, the dentist gets a newsletter that has the success story of another dentist.

Creating this niche newsletter shows the dentist that your product works for <u>THEM</u>, even if it also works for chiropractors.

Customer Attractor #36
Go Out and Make a Speech

In any business the more you get your marketing message out and in front of people, the more you increase your odds of attracting new customers. A great way to get your message out and in front of others is to make presentations to groups of people.

You can go out there and do a talk on almost any topic related to your business. For example, a dentist could do a presentation on "10 things your child must not eat in order to have healthy teeth". A clothing store to talk about "9 ways to get a flat stomach by summer". A carpet cleaner could talk about "How to eliminate spring time allergies" and of course his presentation would talk about the benefits of carpet cleaning and how clean carpets eliminate allergens from the air.

By filling a room with your prospective customers and doing a presentation on a topic that benefits them and that they have an interest in, you're now providing them value. You're also automatically looked upon as an expert or an authority because our society has conditioned us to believe any who does presentations or is an author is an expert.

Customer Attractor #37
Put Yourself In Your
Prospective Customer's Shoes

To attract more customers, you need to think like your customers. Consider that you're an individual looking for the product or service you sell and consider what you would be seeking from a business of your kind.

Answer your own advertising, call your office's toll-free number, try to place an order form your website, etc. Is it an easy process? Does your advertising tell you what you need to know to take the next step? Do you tell your prospects what step to take next?

This could start an entire thought process that may turn up some surprising and hard to swallow results. If you don't uncover anything negative during the process, then you haven't truly placed yourself in your prospective customer's shoes.

This is a great practice to do from time to time. When you work so hard in your business you tend to miss the flaws that are right in front of you.

Customer Attractor #38
Send a Thank You Card

Sending a thank you card to every prospect that inquires about your product, even if they don't buy, speaks volumes for your integrity and the way you do business. It gives you a reason to contact your prospect again, which keeps the relationship going.

You don't have to get fancy. Just a simple card and envelope and write a short message. Simply say "Bob, thanks for coming by the store today. Give me a call if you have any questions. Regards, Michael"

Sending a thank you card tells people that you do not take them for granted and you care about them even if they didn't make a purchase. Taking the time to do little things like sending a thank you can go a long way to building a loyal relationship and attracting new customers.

Customer Attractor #39
Use The Yellow Pages

Yellow Pages can be a very effective advertising medium to spread the word about your business. Though it's not free or even low cost, it's well worth the mention to attract new customers.

Yellow Pages advertising differs from all other medias because it is sold annually. Once you place an ad, your ad stays in it until a year later when that issue of Yellow Pages is replaced with a new edition.

The cost to place your ad varies depending on the kind of ad and listing you go for. Rates also vary depending on the size of the metropolitan area you live in. Running an ad in a small town is less expensive compared to an ad in a major metropolitan area.

If you decide to run an ad in the Yellow Pages there are specific techniques that you can employ to optimize the return on your expense. One technique to keep in mind is to always use direct response marketing techniques when you create you Yellow Pages advertisement.

Customer Attractor #40
Give All Your Staff Business Cards

Your business card makes a statement about your business. It's a statement of what you do and how well you do it. Each employee on your staff is a crucial part of your business and you want them to know that their contribution is important.

To let your employees know that you value them and their contribution to your company, show them you care about them by giving them all business cards. When you do that, you are letting them know that you value them and their contribution.

When all your staff are equipped with business cards and are giving them to everyone them come in contact with, your customers will know that they can approach anyone in your company when they have a question or need assistance.

Customer Attractor #41
Ask For Referrals

Referrals are a great source of new customers. Getting referred to potential customers can be a very effective tool to build your business.

Potential customers that might be hesitant to make a purchase with a company they are unfamiliar with. Referrals give confidence to such prospective customers about the reliability and quality of your product and encourage them to try out your products.

To help solicit referrals from your current customers and business associates, you should clearly explain your product and service offering and define who specifically your ideal customer is. Remember the person making the referral should feel confident enough about your business to recommend your product or service to others.

Who should you be asking for referrals? Here is a short list to get you thinking:

- Your friends

- Vendors and suppliers

- Current customer

- Prospective customer that don't make a purchase but really like you

- Your employees

If you're not comfortable with the idea of asking for referrals, get over it. If you produce a quality product then you should do your best to see that as many people as possible benefit from it.

Customer Attractor #42
Go Viral

The Internet has made getting your message to millions of people fast and economical. What is referred to as "word of mouth" marketing off the Internet is known as viral marketing on the Internet. The term viral is used because the message, like a virus, spreads rapidly from person to person in a very short time.

An effective viral marketing strategy comprises some of the following elements:

- Makes it easy to transfer the information to others

- Exploits common motivations, emotions and behaviors

- Takes advantages of others' resources

Here are a few great methods of spreading you message via viral marketing:

- E-books – by creating a short book in an electronic format such as PDF and giving it away for free, people will want to download it, pass it on to their friends and associates, and add it to their website for others to download.

- Freeware – freeware is a small software application that that you give away for free and is branded with links back to your website. As an example – as a marketing consultant, if I was to create a freeware program, I might create a "Direct Mail ROI Calculator". A small application which would allow people to predict the return on investment of their next direct mail campaign.

- Articles – articles are a great little viral tool. People are always emailing their friends and business associates links to relevant and funny articles they discover on the Internet.

Customer Attractor #43
Post Card Marketing

Using post cards is a very cost effective form of direct mail, especially if your looking to generate new leads and prospects for your business.

Using post cards to market your business has some great advantages:

- Post cards are affordable for almost every business. The cost of the card itself is small, however the postage varies.

- It's easy to track your results. Your post card can tell recipients to bring the card into your store for a special discount. Or it can ask them to use a special ordering code if purchasing from your website.

- Testing an offer with post cards is easy. Just send your card to a small group of people and see how many respond. If you get a good response, now you can feel confident mailing to a larger list.

Post cards make a great marketing tool to attract new customers and market your offers offline.

Customer Attractor #44
Watch The News For PR Opportunities

Public relations (PR) opportunities are a great way to enhance the visibility of your business. PR opportunities can come in many forms like sponsoring an event at a local school, recreation center or church. Such events generally get local publicity and media coverage which would benefit your business.

To seize advantage of such PR opportunities, you should consistently review your local newspapers and news television. Information about such events appear in the media well in advance when the organizers start planning their event.

Customer Attractor #45
Gift Certificates

Gift certificates work well not only to stimulate repeat business from current customers but also to encourage current customer to give them as gifts to their friends and associates.

If you're not using gift certificates in your business, you should. I've seen them work in every type of business imaginable - from coffee shops to book stores to cosmetic surgeons…yes, even cosmetic surgeons are using gift certificates.

Simply by putting up a sign in your store or office that says "Ask about our gift certificates" can lead to thousands of dollars in extra sales per year.

Customer Attractor #46
Article Reprints

Anytime you run a print advertisement or when your business get mentioned favorably in the press, make copies of them and mail these copies to your customers and prospective customers.

With each mailing, include a short cover letter letting them know that you business made news again.

You can also hang them on the wall in your business or enlarge them and place them in a display window.

Customer Attractor #47
Partial Payment Plans

Depending on the price of your product or service, you might want to offer your prospective customers a payment plan or payment options to break up the price into multiple payments.

Say you were offering a $1,000 product, you could offer two payment options:

1. Let them pay in three payment of $333

2. Or payment in full for a 10% book keeping discount

Have some flexibility with this. When talking with your prospects who are having trouble deciding or the ones that decline your offer, ask if a payment plan would help them decide.

Customer Attractor #48
Classified Advertising

Think classified advertising won't work for your business? Give it a try, you'll be amazed at how they work.

Classified advertising is one of the most cost effective marketing mediums any business can use. The advantage that classified advertising has over all other forms of advertising is that people tend to open to the classified section of the newspaper because they have already made a decision to buy.

When you typically run a print ad, you have to convince your prospect to read your ad and then convince them that they need what you're selling. When it comes to classified ads, the people reading them are all ready qualified and are just looking for a deal. All you have to do is get their attention and then get them to deal with you.

To make classified advertising work for you, there are a number of key elements first and the most important is the headline. The headline is the first thing that the reader will notice and is what's going to attract his or her attention to your ad.

The rest of your ad will consist of your offer. You only get one chance with your potential customer, so your first words are critical. Your offer must get your reader interested immediately and compel them to take action to contact you.

One last note, most newspaper offer a wide variety of borders that you can place around your classified ad. A border can help your ad standout but be careful that you don't choose a border that is too elaborate and will get in the way of your offer. The more successful borders are simply a solid or dotted box around your ad.

Customer Attractor #49
Strike While The Iron Is Hot

It's crucial that you act on every quality lead as quickly as possible. Strike while the iron is hot. It's at this moment of truth when your prospect is interested the most.

An interested prospect is expecting exactly what they were promised. They're often eager, enthusiastic and often ready to buy as soon as they hear back from you.

Anticipation is high so the longer you make them wait, the more likely they'll cool off. Or worse…they might forget about you and your offer all-together.

Customer Attractor #50
Create A Unique Selling Proposition

If there's nothing that sets your business apart and gives you a clear advantage over the competition – then what's the point of being in business?

Without something to set you apart or differentiate your business, you're just another option in the marketplace. You need something that will give you an obvious edge over competitors who may have years more experience, name recognition and credibility.

Whenever you do business in a market, you need to offer an appealing alternative. An alternative that offers genuine and lasting benefits so prospects will get a good idea of why they need to do business with you.

Maybe you have the lowest prices in the industry or your market area. If so, that's good. But how much lower are you? How much can your prospects and customers save by buying from you?

Perhaps the support you offer in terms of education, service or marketing assistance is superior to that offered by your competitors.

Or it could be that you offer free shipping, extended hours or better trained salespeople or advisors.

Those are all good things to offer. But, in and of themselves, they don't say much. To use these features for to their fullest advantage, you must quantify them.

Let your prospects and clients know how much lower, how much better, how much superior, how much of an advantage they'll get by doing business with you.

Customer Attractor #51
Use Direct Response Marketing To
Attract New Customers

Direct response marketing is the only form of marketing that allows you to measure and track your Return on Marketing Investment (ROMI). You'll know exactly how many responses each of your lead generating activities bring. Being able to measure the response to your efforts, you'll know immediately how effective your advertisements perform.

By using direct response marketing to attract new customers, you get almost immediate feedback. You get the information you need to determine whether the advertisements are worthwhile to run again. An additional benefit of direct response marketing is that it calls for action and pushes your prospect to respond promptly.

Customer Attractor #52
Start With Small Advertisements

Why start with some big ad when you don't know whether it will be profitable or not. If the ad pulls in new prospects well, you can always run the ad again or increase the size of the ad and run it again.

If you were to listen to the ad rep at the newspaper or magazine, they'll want you to run the biggest ad size they offer. The bigger the better…right? Wrong! In most cases the ad rep just wants a bigger commission check, which they get when you buy a bigger ad.

Customer Attractor #53
Be Original

Most marketplaces are over saturated with advertising in general. Not only is there over saturation but everyone is advertising the same product, the same offer – the same way.

In order to deal with the competition and to catch the eye of your prospects, you have to be interesting. The increasing barrage of advertisements that people are exposed to each day have lead people to develop subconscious filtering devices that allow them to limit their exposure to ads.

However the filtering devices are not foolproof. They might not let ads through but they do let important, interesting, and entertaining things through. When something comes along that pushes someone's emotional "hot button", the filter lets it through and person now has interest towards it.

Customer Attractor #54
Reward Loyalty

How many customers do you have that have been loyalty customers for many years? When was the last time you did something special for them to reward them for their loyalty?

I'm often saddened when I see a client of mine spending so much time and money to lure and attract new business and totally ignore the customers that have been with them for many years.

I'm sure you've seen coupons and offers in advertisements that say "offer valid for new customers only". How would that make you feel if you were a loyal customer to a business for years and you see advertised offers that benefit new customers while you still pay full-price?

I personally think most businesses have it backwards. There's nothing wrong with a great promotion to attract new business but don't ignore your long-time loyalty customers.

Your loyal customers are the ones that are providing you with consistent revenue that allows you to keep the lights on and make payroll. Make them feel appreciated.

Customer Attractor #55
K.I.S.S. Your Prospects

Keep it simple stupid. When it comes to attracting new customers, keep things simple. Create marketing that's straightforward and easily understood, followed by a clear call-to-action.

Your offer is the key information you want to present in your ad and the call-to-action is what you want your prospect to do next. If the ad you've put together requires effort to understand, most of your prospects aren't going to bother.

There are too many other choices in the marketplace for them to bother with your ad. They'll quickly move onto the next message, the next page, the next website, anywhere that they find an easy to understand message.

We're all busier today than ever. If you think your prospects are going to slow down and try to piece together the various bits of information in your ad and try to make sense of it...you're mistaken. It's much easier for them to ignore it and move on...that's exactly what they'll do...move on.

Keep your ad simple. Give them a single focus so that they are easily understood by your target prospects.

Customer Attractor #56
Give Your Prospects a Reason To Respond

If your prospects really want what you're offering they'll find a way to get. It's up to you to create marketing that makes a compelling case for them to want it and give them a reason to take the next step.

Nobody does anything without a reason. If you want your prospects to act, you have to give them a reason...a compelling reason. It must be compelling because not only are you fighting your competition for your prospect's attention, you're also fighting with your prospect's television, cell phone, favorite book, etc.

You have to craft a message that appeals to their emotions, a symptom they're feeling or a cure they're looking for. You need to focus in on whatever it is that weighs heavy on your prospect's mind.

You can create the best advertisement in the world but without action on the part of your prospect, you ad is nothing more than a waste of money. Create a compelling ad by capturing your prospects attention, building interest and the desire for them to take action.

Getting a response is the goal of your lead generation activities and maximizing that response is what we're after. You've got to give them a little push to take action.

Customer Attractor #57
Always Follow-Up

If you've been in business for any amount of time I'm sure you've realized that most prospects don't buy the first time you ask them to. By having a system in place to be able to repeatedly follow-up on unsold prospects, you're practically guaranteed to convert more prospects into customers.

Ideally your goal is to convert as many prospects as you can into customers. The money is in the conversion from prospect to customer. An effective follow-up system can potentially mean thousands of dollars in additional profit in your pocket every month.

Your prospects are busy people. Sometimes you need to light a fire under them to get them to get them to take action. If you consistently keep in touch with your prospects, the more they'll see your marketing message and the more likely that they will respond.

Customer Attractor #58
Cut Your Overhead Expenses –
Not Your Marketing Budget

It amazes me that the first thing a business does when it gets in trouble is they cut their marketing budget. If you're in a position where sales are down and money is tight, the last thing you want to do is to reduce the amount of marketing and advertising you do.

Things happen in every industry. The economy changes and the cost of goods increases, there's not much you can do about that. What you can control is your marketing and the flow of new prospects.

Cut budgets in other areas and redirect the necessary money to marketing. Marketing is what's going to bring in new customers. When money is tight, the trick is to run the marketing campaigns that you know produce results.

By following the guidelines in my marketing system (see www.MichaelAlos.com), you'll understand how to track all your marketing efforts and measure which efforts bring you the greatest return for your marketing dollar. Then run these campaigns while your competition cuts back their marketing budget.

Customer Attractor #59
Show Them The Proof

Never assume your prospects believe the claims you make in advertising copy. Part of a great advertisement is showing proof that your product delivers as you promise.

Here are a few methods you can show proof and back-up all of your claims:

- Testimonials

- Expert endorsements

- Third party tests or studies

- Strong guarantees

- A list of your customers using your product

- Pictures of satisfied customers

If you're advertising a great offer, the proof is just what your prospects might need to make-up their minds as to whether they should buy or not. If you're not already, starting using proof to sell today.

Customer Attractor #60
Use A Toll-Free Recorded Message
To Collect Your Leads

Every time you run an advertisement with your business' phone number in the ad you just might be loosing prospective customers. When you put your business' phone number in the ad, your prospects know that when they call, it's going to be answered by a real live person. Fearing the person answering the phone might give them a sales pitch, your prospect may be apprehensive to call.

By using a toll-free recorded message to greet you prospects, you eliminate their fear of having to talk to a real person and being sold. Toll-free recorded message is simply a voicemail system, with a toll-free number, that is designed specifically for lead generation.

The concept is simple, you publish the toll-free number in your advertisements, your prospects call the number and they are greeted by a message and if they're interested in what you have to offer, they are asked to leave their contact information after the tone.

The message your prospects hear when they call is just a short 60 to 120 second mini commercial on your product or service. During this greeting you present them again with the benefits of your product with the goal of getting the to leave their contact information.

Once they leave their contact information, the voicemail system alerts you via email that someone left a message. You then call and retrieve the message. Once you have their contact information, you can now follow-up with your prospect.

The key to making this Customer Attractor work, is to make sure you let your prospects know they are calling to listen to a recorded message and not a real live person. This can be accomplished by putting the words "call toll-free, 24 hours, 7 days per week, to listen to a recorded message for more information."

Customer Attractor #61
Create Killer Headlines For
Every Advertisement

If you want to instantly increase the response you get from every advertisement your run, then an attention-grabbing headline is vital! In marketing tests that I've conducted in my own business, I've notice one advertisement out-pull another by as much 1800% just by adding or changing headline.

I don't think I can emphasize the importance of including a headline in your ads enough. Over 5 times as many people will read your ad simply because your ad has a headline. Not just any headline will work. It has to catch the attention of your target prospect and make them want to read the rest of your advertisement.

There is no magic formula for writing an attention-grabbing headline but here are a few guidelines:

- It has to absolutely stop your target prospect in their tracks and force them to read your ad

- It must answer the question "What's in it for me" by giving your products best benefit right up front

- It has to set the tone for the entire rest of the ad and your offer

On the next page, you'll find a shorted copy of my "Headline Checklist" to aid you in writing headlines for your advertisements.

Headline Checklist

☐ Does your headline draw your targeted audience to attention?

☐ Does your headline list your biggest benefit?

☐ Does your headline answer the "What's In It For Me" Question?

☐ Is your headline believable?

☐ Does it make you want to read the entire message now?

☐ Did you add quotation marks around it?

☐ Did you check to make sure it was "YOU" focused?

☐ Did you use both upper and lower case letters?

☐ Did you consider using a picture to the right of the headline?

☐ Have you tried "Quickly and Easily" in it?

☐ Have you tried "...100% Guaranteed" on the end of it?

Customer Attractor #62
Close Your Prospects

Any salesperson in the world will tell you they typically spend the most time on trying to close their prospect. A close is part of a sale where you actually ask them to buy or make a purchase from you.

There are thousands of books filled with word-for-word scripts of the various closes that can be used to get someone buy. Even with all the information out there on closing, 90% of the businesses doing any advertising at all don't do anything to close their prospects.

If you can't close, you can't sell. If you don't sell, you don't make any money. There's nothing wrong with asking someone to buy once you've presented him or her with all the information they need to make a decision.

Generally a close is built around these 3 elements:

1. Scarcity or the take-away

2. Warning

3. Take action now

To close, let your prospect know that they need to take action now while supplies last. Or that in three weeks the prices will increase.

You'll be surprised how many more sales you make just by asking your prospect if they want to buy.

To aid you in formulating your close, I have included an abbreviated version of my Closing Checklist.

Closing Checklist

☐ Did you tell your prospects how scarce your product is?

☐ Did you explain to them why they have to order now?

☐ Did you tell them every way they could order?

☐ Did you give them instructions for phone ordering?

☐ Did you give them instructions for fax ordering?

☐ Did you give them instructions for mail ordering?

☐ Did you warn them about not ordering your product?

☐ Did you tell them what benefits they will miss out on?

☐ Did you make it more painful to them to stay in the status quo then to pull out their checkbooks?

☐ Did you tell them they have to order now?

☐ Did you tell them the benefit of ordering now?

☐ Did you restate the offer and deadline when closing?

Customer Attractor #63
Test, Test, Test

You finally get an advertisement or direct mail sales letter that starts to attract new customers. What then? Are you done with your marketing efforts?

You may think that you're done because your ad seems to be working…but the fact is, you are far from done. In fact, your marketing is never done. It will always need improvement. All good sales people know that no matter how good they are, there is always need for improvement.

All your marketing pieces will always have room for improvement. You'll need to consistently test them. Create new ones and test them against the pieces that are currently attracting new customers.

Testing is never complete. You should always be testing headlines. Testing one advertisement against another. Testing your close. Testing what media you run your ads in. Don't be fooled, even the big companies still test to improve their return on marketing investment.

So how do you test your ads? By 'keying' your ads. Keying is what is referred to when you mark your ad so that you know where the lead is coming from. If you don't key your ad, you'll never know which ad is bringing in the leads and which ones are the poor performers.

One way to key your ads is usually by adding a department number or a specific telephone extension. When your prospect responds, they ask or write to that department.

If your prospect is responding by mail, your ad would look like this:

Growth Publications
824 S. 3rd Street, Dept. # R3
Philadelphia, PA 19147

The 'key' in the address above is the "R3". There is not a R3 location at this address, it's a code that allows me to match the response to the advertisement and the paper or magazine I ran the ad in.

If I ran an add and asked the responder to call my toll-free number, it might look something like this:

1-800-000-0000 ext 3

The 'key' in the above example is the "extension 3". Each advertisement I place in a paper would have a different extension. I know exactly which ad and where the ad was run if someone calls my office via extension 3. Virtual mailboxes have made "keying" ads like this very affordable.

Customer Attractor #64
Search The Help Wanted Advertisements

Here's a customer attraction strategy that's very stealth and not used by many businesses. Every day there are thousands of companies advertising their available employment positions. What most businesses that sell business-to-business don't realize is that these employment ads offer a huge opportunity to attract new customers.

The opportunities come not from the employment ad itself, but from what you can infer from the ad. When you read the ad it's obvious what position they are trying to fill. If the employment ad says "sales manager wanted" then you know that they are looking for, a sales manager.

What you want to look at is what's not stated in the ad. What can you infer from a company that's hiring a sales manager or additional sales staff? What products or services might a company hiring sales staff need?

It might be a logical assumption, that if they are hiring sales staff, that the company doing the hiring, might be a great candidate for a sales training program, a customer relationship management software, sales incentives and rewards, etc.

Three great sources of employment ads on the Internet are:

1. CareerBuilder.com

2. HotJobs.com

3. Monster.com

Keep an eye out for companies that are recruiting for positions that either influence or make the decision to buy the types of products or services that your business offers.

Customer Attractor #65
Customer Lists of Your Competitors

Many businesses publish a list of their customers on their website. This is very common in the business-to-business world. These customer lists can be a great source to find new leads for your prospecting efforts.

Visit the websites of all your direct competitors (or even businesses that offer products that complement yours). Do they have a listing of all their customers? If not, look and see if they have testimonials from their customers. You might even find in some cases the names of a decision maker in the company will be listed in the testimonial.

Now, thanks to the customer list or testimonials on their websites, you now who some of their customers are. If you've done any competitive research, you know how your business stacks up against your competitor.

You know who your competition's customers are, you know your competitive advantage, now you just need to put your customer attraction strategy into action and get your foot in the door.

Customer Attractor #66
Attracting More Customers With Contests

Contests are a great way to attract new customers to your store or website. Holding regular contests on a weekly or monthly basis can be a great way to generate a consistent flow of new leads.

A great advantage of holding a contest is that people have to fill out an entry form. In order to be entered into the contest, the form must be completed. A completed entry form can contain a great deal of information about your prospective customer.

When you create your entry form, be sure to put some thought into what information you want to collect. Sure you want your prospect's contact information but you might also want to collect some data that will further qualify them as a candidate for what you are selling.

Another great way to use contests is to let your prospects and current customers know who the winner was. Make it a big deal that they won and what the prize was. People hate to feel like they missed out and didn't win. This may work to solicit further involvement for future contests.

Customer Attractor #67
Use A Lead Management System
To Keep Track Of Leads

I've seen a statistic somewhere that stated that less than 4% of sales are closed on the first call. It takes an average of seven to nine impressions of your marketing message to get a cold prospect ready to buy. That's why follow-up is a critical part of your selling process.

In order to keep track of each prospect and where they are in your sales process, you should consider some form of software system to keep track of your leads and prospective customers. There are many approaches to developing a follow-up system, just keep in mind to use what works for you and your business.

Depending on the size of your business, you might be able to get away with using index cards to keep track of your prospects. You can start by just putting your prospect's contact information on the card and segmenting the cards by the product that your prospect is interested in.

For more established businesses, a customer relationship management (CRM) system is what you should be using as your lead management system. CRM is a software application that helps companies understand, as well as anticipate, the needs of current and potential customers.

For more detailed information on CRM systems and their functionality, below are the leaders in CRM for the small and medium sized business market:

- Salesforce.com

- SageCRMSolutions.com

- Act.com

- Crm.Dymanics.com (Microsoft)

Customer Attractor #68
Know Your Ideal Customer

Are you clear about who exact your ideal customers are? Many businesses make the mistake of trying to appeal to everyone that could use their product or service. This approach is what I call the "shot gun" approach, i.e. marketing to anyone and everyone who might buy your product

When a business uses the "shot gun" approach, they typically figure that sales is a numbers game. If their sales people set enough appointments and ask enough people to buy, eventually someone will say 'yes'.

When you clarify who your ideal customer is, it'll suddenly become more clear where to find them and how to market to them. You can develop messages that appeal directly to them. And because you've narrowly defined your ideal customer, you'll also be able to improve your product or service so that your customers are getting the most value.

When you have a clear picture of who your ideal customer is, who can develop a marketing message that's specifically for them and easily understood by them. You're actually able to send your message to fewer numbers of prospects and get an even greater response.

Now ask yourself, who exactly is your ideal customer? Where are they? What industry are they in? What size business do they run? What are they looking for? What's they're buying process? Why would they want what you have to offer?

With a clear description of your ideal customer, you'll be able to increase the return on your marketing investment and have a well-defined niche to prospect. This alone will make attract new customer quicker and easier.

Customer Attractor #69
Use "Grabbers" On All Your Direct Mail
To Make Your Letters Grab
Your Prospect's Attention

Research shows that up to 65% of mail never reaches the person it's intended for. By making use of grabbers, you increase your chances of getting your mail into the hands of the person it was intended for.

A grabber is a term coined by the direct mail industry. It's essentially an item attached to your direct mail letter that is meant to "grab" your prospect's attention. Some of types of items you can attach to your direct mail are:

- Aspirin

- Teabags

- Money and coins

- Scratch lottery tickets

- Rubber balls

- Fake checks

The objective to using a grabber is to attract the attention of your prospect and make your letter memorable to your prospect. There's nothing more memorable to someone than receiving a teabag attached to a letter in the mail.

To really make this strategy work, just attaching the grabber isn't enough, you have to tie the grabber into your marketing message. Typically you would link your opening sentence and headline to the grabber.

For example, in the case of using an aspirin on your letter:

Your headline might read: "Are outdated and costly marketing mistakes giving you a headache?"

Then the first sentence of your letter might read: "You may have noticed that I've attached an aspirin to this letter." And you may be wondering why I have done this…"

Then your letter goes onto explain further on why the aspirin was attached and how you or your business can solve their headaches.

Customer Attractor #70
Begin With Your Goal In Mind

Before you embark on any new customer attraction program, first you need to map out your entire lead generation and selling process. By starting with your end-result in mind, you'll be able to work backwards and choose a customer attraction strategy that'll help you best achieve your goal.

Here are a few key questions to ask yourself during the planning stage:

- What's the ultimate goal of your lead generation program (how many new customers do you need)?

- On average, how many appointments or sales presentations do you need to get one new customer?

- How many marketing pieces (or advertisements) do you need to run to generate one qualified lead (your response rate)?

- How many leads can your sales force handle at one time, in terms of qualifying and follow-up?

Of course, there's a lot more to it than that but try to get an understanding of the numbers before you start. You may not know how many leads it takes to generate one sale, but you may know how many appointments you need to generate one sale. Dividing the number of appointments by the number of new customers will give you a rough conversion rate.

Customer Attractor #71
Recycle Your Leads

Here's a great little and under-utilized strategy that'll easily increase the return on investment of all of your marketing campaigns by 20% to 50%. Simply take any leads that didn't buy and any lost sales opportunities and funnel them back into your customer attraction system.

The reason for recycling leads is simple - timing is everything. Just because they didn't respond or didn't buy the first time around doesn't mean they won't buy now. Conditions in their business might have changed, things in their life might have changed, by following-up with these leads now just might land you a few new customers.

In many cases, by putting these 'old' prospects into a follow-up sequence will result in sales. You can convert those prospects who decided to put off their purchase initially. You also have a great chance of converting prospects who might have decided to buy from your competitor but because your competition isn't following-up, you'll get the next sale.

Customer Attractor #72
Pre-Selling Your Product Or Service

If you have a product or service that lends itself to repeat purchases, you can pre-sell it at a special price. Think of pre-selling as offering your customer a discount if they buy a specific quantity of your product at one time.

To better illustrate the concept, here are a few examples:

• Dentists can offer one year's worth of cleanings or a family pack of services for a flat fee.

• Restaurants can offer a pre-paid number of lunches or dinners at a reduced advance price. This can even be done with carryout.

• Lawn mowing or landscaping can offer a 12-month service for the price of 10 months if paid in full.

• A car wash can offer a wax and detail (worth $25) with every 5 car washes paid in advance.

• A café can sell a monthly coffee card where customers pay for a full-month's (30 days worth) for the price of 25 days worth of coffee.

• A Laundromat can offer free drying with every wash, if you purchase 10 washes in advance.

• Delicatessens can offer "deli-dollars" purchased in advance at a discount that can be used to purchase meals.

Pre-selling your product or service is a terrific way to get an immediate increase in cash. Utilizing this strategy, you're getting your customers to pay you today for services that you won't render until a later date.

Customer Attractor #73
Keep Running Ads That Work

If you want to keep a steady stream of new customers coming, don't stop running advertisements that work. Never change any advertisement that's working for you until you've got something better to replace it with.

The way you make money in any business is by creating a system around the activities that make you the most money and let the system run over and over again. If you keep creating and changing your advertisements, you're essentially working against yourself and hurting your profits in the process.

You have to set your goals and test your ideas but don't stop running ads that are working for you. Even if you've been running the ad for years, as long as the ad continues to bring in new customers, keep it going.

You'll find that you'll get tired of seeing the same ad in the newspaper week after week long before your prospects will. A word of warning, evening the direct marketing pros make this mistake. They'll have a 'control ad', an ad that produces predictable leads each time they run it, and they stop running the ad. Not because the ad stopped pulling in new leads but because they got tired of seeing it.

Make sure you never stop running the ads that produce the greatest results for your business.

Customer Attractor #74
Learn To Write Advertising Copy

Anyone can create an advertisement but not anyone can create an advertisement that can cost effectively attracts new customers. The scope of creating ads the can consistently attract new customers is a large endeavor and is deserving of an entire book itself.

There's good news, I'm going to reveal a great little shortcut to writing effective ad copy. All good print ads and sales letters are "salesmanship in print". That means if you took the words you would use to sell your product to someone while face-to-face with them and put them in an ad or on paper, you now have "salesmanship in print".

That shortcut is to have someone else interview you and ask you questions about your product or service. When going through a questioning process, typically the highlights of your product jump out at your. These highlights are the major elements that you need to include in your advertisements.

Simply grab your top performing sales person(s) or some who has great success in selling your product and interview them thoroughly. During the interview have them sell the product or service to you while you tape record the conversation. If you interview your top 3 to 5 sales people, not only will you make sure you get all the sales elements but you also confirm the most important elements.

Once you've conducted all the interviews, you'll have to have the tapes transcribed. Once transcribed, read through them looking for the common highlights to jump out at you. These highlights are the elements you want to include in your advertisements.

By no means are you finished at this point, but it's a start. You'll still have to add a headline, testimonials, the close and other elements of the ad or sales letter.

To make the interviewing process easier for you, I've included a few sample questions at the end of this chapter that you can use to start the interview process.

Copywriting Questions

Below is a list of 15 questions to assist you in developing advertisements that sell. Refer to this list every time before you begin to write any ad or sales letter.

1. What is the goal of your copy?

_____

_____

_____

_____

_____

2. What is the overall goal you're trying to achieve? Look to the future (6 months from now). If this project could accomplished by completing just one critical task, what would that be?

_____

_____

_____

_____

_____

3. What product or service will you be selling?

_____

_____

_____

_____

4. Is there anything about your product or company that lends

credibility to your sales pitch? (This could include awards you've won, how long you've been in business, how many locations you have, etc.)

_____

_____

_____

_____

_____

5. What are all the features of your product? (Don't leave anything out.)

_____

_____

_____

_____

_____

6. What relevant facts and figures have been gathered about your product? For example:

    a. Have any studies been made that provide facts and figures that will substantiate your claims?

    _____

    _____

    _____

    b. Is there an industry resource that can give you meaningful facts, graphs, charts and statistics about your product?

    _____

    _____

    _____

    c. How does your product compare to your competitor's

products?

_____

_____

_____

7. What are the major benefits your customer gets from your
    product? (The difference between a fact/feature and a
    benefit is this: a fact/feature is something the product does, a
    benefit is something it does for your customer).

_____

_____

_____

_____

_____

8. What major benefits do your customers get from doing
    business with you, rather than doing business with your
    competition?

_____

_____

_____

_____

_____

9. What major benefits do your customers get from your
    product, rather than your competition's products? Develop
    your 'unique selling proposition' (USP). What makes doing
    business with you "unique"? Why should a prospect favor
    you with their business instead of your competition?

_____

_____

10. What is your customer's main reason for needing your product or service?

_____

_____

_____

_____

11. Create a short, accurate profile of the type of customer you'd most like to attract.

_____

_____

_____

_____

_____

12. What type of guarantee do you offer?

_____

_____

_____

_____

13. What level of service and support do you offer?

_____

_____

_____

_____

_____

14. Collect and analyze the marketing pieces and items listed below:

• Sales letters	• Back issues of promotional newsletters
• Newspaper and magazine ads	
• Radio and television spots	• Classified ads
	• Marketing plans
• Brochures	• Market research
• Catalogues	• Product sample(s)
• Press kits and news releases	• Testimonial letters from satisfied customers
• Telemarketing scripts	
• Sales training materials	• Complaint letters from dissatisfied customers

15. Finally, "sell" your product to a customer as if they were sitting across the table from you.

_____

_____

_____

_____

_____

_____

_____

Customer Attractor #75
Joint Ventures To Attract New Customers

Joint ventures (JV) are an excellent idea and a great way to leverage the resources of other business. Joint ventures are a very simple and powerful marketing tool. However less than 5% of businesses are using some form of JV. In reality, a joint venture is very simple to setup and they're based on the business rule that says, "People like to buy from someone they know and trust."

Joint ventures are extremely profitable when you consider the lifetime value of a customer. It can cost as much as five to six times more to get a new customer than to resell to an existing customer. It costs less and less every time a current customer makes a purchase from you. The costs decrease because you don't have to pay any advertising expense to reach them.

A joint venture is a form of partnership where two businesses come together to share knowledge, experience, markets, profits and customers. Joint ventures take on numerous forms and arrangements. Here's an example:

Company A agrees to let Company B deliver a sales message to people who are Company A's customers. In the sales message, Company A endorses the products or service that Company B offers. If you were Company B in this joint venture, the JV would bring you new customer and sales more quickly.

Sales come easier in this case because Company A has endorsed Company B. Since Company A's customer trust Company A, the endorsement is a sure way to break down any fear or skepticism that one might have about the quality of Company B's products. Eliminating the fear of the unknown with an endorsement leads to more sales for Company B.

See Bonus Section #3 in this book for more benefits and strategies for using joint ventures.

Examples Of Joint Venture Partnerships

1. Auto detailer / car dealership / car wash / car parts store / auto insurance company

2. Beautician / tanning salon / sunglass store / beauty products

3. Boarding kennel / pet groomer / pet product vendor

4. Bookstore / publisher / self publisher

5. Bridal store / wedding photographer / wedding planner / printer / limo service / florist

6. Chiropractor / health supplement vendor / health product manufacturer

7. Construction company / architectural firm / interior designer / landscaper

8. Doctors / drug companies / health supplement companies / pharmacists

9. Dentist / tooth whitening products / pharmacists

10. Dry cleaner / restaurant catering to power-lunching businesspeople

11. Florist / candy store / funeral parlor / restaurants

12. Golf pro shop / golf instruction video producer / golf instructor

13. Graphic designer / printer / copy writer

14. Gym / karate instructor / nutritional supplements

15. House painter / carpenter / carpet store / appraiser

16. Landscaper / lawn care service / plant nursery / garden supply store

17. Law firm / financial consultant / accountant

18. Moving company / packaging store / storage facility

19. Plumber / electrician / carpenter / handy man

20. Real estate agent / security company / doctors / carpet companies / restaurant

21. Resort hotel / seminar presenter

22. Restaurant / radio station

23. Tailor / jeweler

Customer Attractor #76
Market To Your Past Customers

If you've been in business for any length of time and you already have a customer base, you should make it a priority to focus on internal marketing. That means marketing to any of your previous customers who have not done business with you in a while.

While this book is about attracting more new customers, most businesses tend to focus solely on attracting new customers and often forget about the great potential for more business that exists already in their customer database.

Why should you market to your list of past and current customers?

First of all, it's the least expensive form of marketing that you can do. Marketing to past customers is five times more effective that trying to attract new customers. Since they've already done business with you in the past, you already have built trust and rapport with them, leaving them more likely to respond to any marketing message they receive from you.

Your past customers are already qualified since they have bought from your before. You know they can afford what it is your offer and that they have an interest in doing business with you. That is, if their previous experience with your was a satisfactory one.

If all that doesn't convince you to market to your past customers then maybe this will…your past customers can be a great source of referrals. There's nothing more powerful than getting someone to refer and endorse your business to others.

Customer Attractor #77
Bring In a Marketing Consultant
For Fresh Ideas

Once you've been in business for a few years your marketing is bound to get stale and boring and your prospects will become totally immune to your marketing message. Engaging someone who can offer and implement new marketing strategies cannot only generate new customers but also be very profitable.

Often, when working with a new client, I recommend an excellent idea and my client often wonders why they never thought of it themselves. The reason is most business owners are too close to the business and spend too much time working in their business. This is exactly what prevents you from making your business as profitable as it can be.

A marketing consultant can also provide stimulation by asking you the right questions and getting your brain working. Questioning your thought process can make all the difference to in the direction you take your business.

When you do pursue a marketing consultant, look for someone who is a good listener and is capable of asking thought-provoking and challenging questions. Your consultant should work with you to arrive at the best possible solution to achieve your business growth goals.

To speak to me about whether my consulting services would be a fit for your business, contact me via my website, www.MichaelAlos.com.

Business Growth Questions

It's been stated that 95% of businesses simply use one method of attracting new customers. Typically they've been using this one method ever since they've been in business.

The following questions are thought provoking questions to get you to start thinking about what you're currently doing to attract new customers and how you can expand to more than one method

1. What marketing activity is currently attracting the most new customers for my business?

   Answering this question will help you focus on doing more of the most profitable activity that's growing your business. Aim to do whatever it is that gives you the greatest return for the least amount of money and hassle.

   _____

   _____

   _____

   _____

   _____

   _____

   _____

   _____

2. What else can I do to increase the part of my business that's the most profitable - without having to work any harder?

   _____

   _____

   _____

   _____

   _____

3. In what other ways can I benefit or profit from the relationship I already have with my customers?

    This may include, but is not limited to asking for referrals, up-selling another product, promoting other people's products, asking to make another purchase, etc.

    _____

    _____

    _____

    _____

    _____

    _____

    _____

4. Who already deals with my ideal customer and is in the best position to recommend me to them? Who could I joint venture with?

    In a joint venture, you leverage the relationship someone has already built with their customers. It allows you to tap into this relationship, which they built over their years in business.

    _____

    _____

    _____

    _____

    _____

    _____

    _____

5. Who else stands to benefit most by me growing my business and getting more sales?

Here you're looking for people like your suppliers, investors, vendors, partners, and so on. By focusing on this question you'll be able to enlist their help and support in growing your business. They'll also reap the benefit as your business grows.

_____

_____

_____

_____

_____

_____

_____

6. How can I reduce the risk and increase the attractiveness of my offer to attract more new customers into my business?

We've already talked about the benefits of eliminating the risk for first-time buyers. A great way to do this is by offering a guarantee or a free trial.

_____

_____

_____

_____

_____

_____

_____

Bonus Section #1

7 Marketing Mistakes That Destroy Business Profits

How To Fix These Mistakes Before They Ruin Your Business
Using Simple & Easy Strategies

Almost every business that I have consulted with has been guilty of making 7 major marketing mistakes. I haven't kept score, but I would have to guess that these 7 marketing mistakes are costing a business hundreds-of-thousands, if not, millions of dollars in lost profits each year.

My guess, you're probably making these same 7 mistakes. But by the end of this bonus section, you'll have the know-how to put your business back on the path-to-profits.

Even if you focus solely on only one mistake and eliminate it completely from your business, you'll catapult your business past your competition. Eliminate them all and the sky's the limit!

Marketing Mistake #1 - Failure To Let Your Prospects And Customers Know The Unique Benefits They Get From Doing Business With You And Not Your Competitors

"Why should I do business with you, instead of all the other options I have?"

This is by far the most common mistake businesses make today. You see, your prospective customers are exposed to thousands upon thousands of advertisements from your competitors and other businesses each day. Right now, I bet they're asking "why should I do business with you, instead of all the other options available?"

This IS a question that goes through each of your prospect's minds before they choose to do business with you. They may do it consciously or they might not ever be aware that they are asking themselves the question. Either way, the question, "why should I do business with you, instead of all the other options available?", is running through their mind and being used to make their decision.

It doesn't matter what product or service is being offered, your customers can go nearly anywhere and find the exact same (or very similar) products or services offered for the same price, or perhaps for even less money than what you charge.

So why should they come to your business and do business with you?

Think about that question for a minute. Now ask yourself, "why do you do shop at the same stores or eat at the same restaurants over and over again?"

Most likely, it's because they offer you something you can't get from their competitors. Maybe they're closer to where you live or work.

Or maybe you like the way a particular restaurant prepares a certain meal. Perhaps it's the environment or the people who work there. It may not be one single thing that influences you, but rather a combination of several factors.

Nevertheless, the businesses you continue to frequent give you something special. Something unique. Something you just can't get anywhere else. It's that uniqueness that keeps you coming back over and over again.

If you expect your prospects to do business with you rather than your competition, you must have something that sets you apart from the rest of your competitors.

This "something" that sets you apart, is known as your Unique Selling Proposition or USP.

Without a clearly defined factor that differentiates you or sets your business apart from everyone else who offers the same (or similar) products or services as you, your business will be no different than any other business your clients or prospects will encounter, and there will be no reason for others to do business with you rather than your competitors.

On the other hand, a well thought-out, carefully identified USP can differentiate you and your business and make you stand out from your competition as unique, different, and special, and the business that's most desirable to do business with.

Coming up with your own USP doesn't have to be difficult. It's simply a matter of identifying what you have to offer your clients, customers or prospects beyond what the product or service you offer can provide.

Let's look at what's probably the most well known USP of all time:

"Red hot pizza delivered to your door in 30 minutes or less – guaranteed" ~ Dominos Pizza

This was the USP for Dominos Pizza. Dominos became a billion dollar enterprise with the help of this USP. Tom Monahan, the founder of Dominos, recognized that in order to win in the pizza business, he had to be different.

Don't worry if you we can't think of anything that creates a significant difference between you and your competitors. Your USP can be about anything or any area that sets you apart from your competition.

Do you have longer or more convenient hours? Do you have a better guarantee? Do you offer a wider selection? Is your staff certified or professionally trained?

You must find a unique advantage that your business has over your competitors. But there's a little secret to creating a USP and separating your business from your competition.

Most businesses say things like, "Family Owned for 5 Generations", "The Most Reliable Service", "Lowest Prices Guaranteed", "Satisfaction Guaranteed", "Board Certified" or something like "We use quality ingredients".

These statements are pretty much meaningless and do nothing to set your business apart. Not only can most of your competitors say the same things, they do say them. Instead, you want to be very clear about how the advantages you offer will benefit your customers.

Tell them exactly what they can expect from you. It may be that you only offer your customers, clients and prospects the highest quality, "top-of-the-line" products. If so, that's great. But tell them in very specific, definable and quantifiable terms so they understand exactly what "highest quality, top-of-the-line" means to them, and how they'll benefit.

Maybe you have the lowest prices in the industry or your market area. If so, that's good. But how much lower are you? How much can your prospects and customers save by buying from you?

Perhaps the support you offer in terms of education, service or marketing assistance is superior to that offered by your competitors.

Or it could be that you offer free shipping, extended hours or better trained salespeople or advisors.

Those are all good things to offer. But, in and of themselves, they don't say much. To use these features for to their fullest advantage, you must quantify them.

Show your prospects and clients very clearly how much lower, how much better, how much superior, how much of an advantage they'll get by doing business with you.

Spell out exactly, clearly and specifically what advantages and benefits your customers will gain. Whatever you choose to make your USP, remember, it must be perceived as desirable to your prospects and customers. In other words, they have to consider it to be of value to them.

Developing an effective USP doesn't have to be difficult or time-consuming. But it absolutely must be done if you expect to gain and maintain any kind of an advantage in today's marketplace.

Marketing Mistake #2 - Using Institutional Or Image Advertising Instead of Emotional Direct Response Advertising

Advertising is simply the process of letting others know about your product or service. Institutional or image advertising is the type of advertising most companies, large and small use most often.

While institutional or image advertising can alert your prospects to the fact that your product exists, it does very little to create a desire in the minds of the buying public to own the product, or at least inquire for more information concerning the product.

A better, more effective and more cost-efficient form of advertising, is called "direct response" advertising.

The idea behind direct response advertising is to compel the reader to take some specific action. Either make a call or visit a web site or some other action.

The only goal of direct response advertising is to get the reader to take action or to do something. Take the action or do something that will lead to a sale or purchase of your product or service.

Institutional or image advertising is fine if all you want to do is promote the image of your company, your products, or the services you offer.

But when you consider the fact that your client or prospect couldn't care less about your company or the fact that you want to sell them something, it adds up to a big waste of your money... money that could be better utilized elsewhere.

It's true that institutional or image advertising can help build "brand-awareness." And that's okay for large corporations that have multi-million dollar advertising budgets. But most small or medium size businesses simply cannot afford to spend their advertising dollars this way.

Most institutional advertising is not customer-focused. Instead, it promotes how great the company paying for the ad is. And since there is no call to action, at best, the results this kind of advertising produces are deferred results.

For the most part, people don't care about how great your company is. They really care more about what a particular product or service can do for them.

They have their own wants and needs that they want to satisfy, and they will only buy what you are offering if you can show them how your product or service will satisfy those wants and needs.

That's where emotional direct response advertising comes in.

This type of advertising shows the reader the advantages your product or service can provide them and let them know exactly what steps they must take to either get the product or service, or to get more information about it.

Emotional direct response is designed to present enough information to give a compelling and immediate reason for the viewer to take some specific action. To send in a coupon, pick up the phone and call for an order or more information, or to stop by your place of business.

Another great benefit of using direct response advertising is the results of the advertisement can be tracked and measured. Direct response advertising allows all your advertising to be held accountable. That means, you'll be able to quantify exactly how many dollars you pay out for your marketing efforts, where your results come from and how many dollars you bring in as a result.

Direct-response advertising is simply the most effective type of marketing for most businesses, and effectively used, can bring immediate profits to your bottom line.

Marketing Mistake #3 - Using Failure To Monitor Your Results

Results! That's all that counts in business. Results!

Any advertising or marketing promotion worth putting your time, money and effort behind, is worth measuring how well it performs. Only by knowing what kinds of results a certain marketing effort produces, can you determine whether or not to run it again, or what you may need to do to change or tweak it in order to make it more effective.

It's absolutely amazing how many business owners don't understand this simple concept. They'll let the Yellow Pages advertising salesperson sell them an ad in their local book, let the Yello w Pages ad department layout the ad, then let the ad run with no way of knowing whether or not a prospect called or a customer was obtained as a result of that ad.

The ad has no "accountability" or "measurability." So, next year, the same ad gets run, the same results are had, and the business owner continues to complain about how poor business is.

And the same thing happens with his or her newspaper ads, magazine ads, direct mail campaigns, Val-Pak marketing and every other type of marketing they do.

As an astute business person, you should never even consider running an ad or executing a mailing campaign or promotion without having some type of response mechanism to measure the results.

You wouldn't think of ordering and paying for a product…any kind of product, and then not checking to see if you received it.Yet, many business owners will run ads in their newspaper, magazines, Money Mailer, or Val-Pak, or send out a mailing and never even bother to see what kind of results the ad produced.

I know it's crazy. But it happens every day. And millions of dollars are wasted because of it.

Some people even go so far as to say, "Well, my advertising isn't to bring in customers right away. Its purpose is to keep our name in front of our prospects and create 'top-of-mind-awareness' so when they're ready, they'll remember me."

Well, top of mind awareness is important. There's no question about that. But you can't afford to operate your business on "deferred results."

Each of your ads and mailings must have a definite, targeted purpose. And each ad must be measured to see that it, in fact, does accomplish that purpose. The purpose might be to get them to make a call, to complete a survey, to place an order or some other form of action.

You can use any system to measure the results of each and every advertising or promotion campaign you run. I often recommend my clients purchase my "Advertising and Promotion Results Analysis" program. Which comes with binder packed with analysis forms, a special report on how to prepare your advertisements so they can be trackable and a compact disc containing a spreadsheet that performs the profit and loss calculations for you.

Regardless of what system you use, add up all the costs incurred to create and launch the campaign. Determine how many sales that results from the campaign. Then subtract what profit that was made.

This explanation was simplified, but I hope you get the picture. If you're interested in learning more about how to track and measure your marketing, contact me for more information of my "Advertising and Promotion Results Analysis" program.

Marketing Mistake #4 - Not Profiting From the Lifetime Value of Your Customers

One of the greatest mistakes that businesses make is failing to see beyond the first transaction a customer makes with them. Businesses are in such a hurry to go out and get more new customers, they overlook a very profitable asset sitting right in front of them.

Here's what I mean...

Let's say on the first sale of a new customer, the customer buys your product or service which costs $1,000. Your gross margin after delivering your service is 50%, which means you make $500 per new customer.

However, it cost you $600 to generate this one new customer (the total cost of your advertising) so you actually made a loss of $100 on this first sale. If you're one of the few businesses that actually measure the results of your advertising, based on these assumptions, you'd probably conclude that this approach was not profitable and you'd stop using it.

That's how 99% of business people evaluate their success – based on the first transaction or sale. Nearly every business spends more money, time and effort to the acquisition of new customers than they do to keep their existing customers.

Studies have proven time and time again, that it costs more than five times as much to bring a new customer on board than it does to retain existing customers and to get them to make additional purchases.

What's interesting is that most business owners can tell you almost to the penny, what the value of their furniture, fixtures and equipment is, as well as how much money they have tied up in stock and inventory.

But, when it comes to the most valuable asset they have... their customers, they don't have any clue as to what they are worth.

Now in most businesses, the customer keeps coming back for more. However this is usually a result of the customer deciding to come back, not the business owner soliciting the customer to come back. Getting a customer to keep doing business with you over a specific time period means the customer is actually worth much more to you than the amount generated on the first transaction.

This in effect is what's known as Lifetime Customer Value.

Lifetime Customer Value is the average profit a customer generates during the duration of the relationship with you.

Let's revisit the above example to again to further illustrate this concept...

Now, let's say one new customer generates the same $1,000 per year but they pay make purchases of $1,00 every year, for 5 years. Your gross margin for delivering your service is the same 50%.

That now means by looking at the value over the duration of the relationship, the average lifetime value is $1,900 ($5,000 x 50% = $2,500 – Cost of advertising $600) and not -$100 like we had in the first example! Plus these figures don't include any referrals the customer will also bring!

Do you see the difference? All it takes is a simple shift in thinking, and you can leverage your business so much that it astonishes your competition.

Well now you know what each customer is worth to you, it means you can actually spend more money to acquire the customer in the first place.

Marketing Mistake #5 - Not Cross-Selling, Up-Selling Or Having A "Back-End"

Marketing your business can be costly. Even if you understand the numbers and the principle of Lifetime Customer Value, it's still going to require that you spend some money to get prospects coming through the door.

Unfortunately, businesses that don't understand how to cost-effectively market their business, look at spending money on marketing as a negative, or an expense, thus they don't aggressively engage in it. But marketing doesn't have to be a business expense. It can really be an investment... an investment that returns a significant amount of profits to you, if you understand and approach it properly.

It's true that in most cases, it's easier and it costs less to sell additional products and services to your existing customers than it does to new prospects. Studies show that it costs up to five times more to sell to a new customer versus an existing one.

In many instances, businesses actually lose money on each new customer they attract, because the costs of marketing exceed the profits they make on the first sale. That's why the principle of Lifetime Customer Value is so crucial to the success or failure of a business.

Luckily for us, there is a way to help us increase the Lifetime Customer Value of all your customers. If you want your business to grow...really grow...and do it in the least painful way, and with maximum results and minimum costs, you need to establish a systematic way to get people to upgrade their purchases and/or to buy additional products.

At great time to ask your customer to buy an additional product is at the point of purchase. By asking your customers while they are currently in the middle of a pruchase, you'll increase your odds of successfully selling them an additional product or service.

"Bundling," "Packaging," "Cross-selling" and "Up-selling" are just a few examples of how you might provide additional products or services to your customers at the time of purchase.

Any upgrades or additional sales you make in this manner are pure profit, since no advertising costs or other overhead expenses were incurred to create the sale. By incorporating this one simple step into your sales process, you can increase your sales amount per customer significantly, and really boost your bottom line.

Now, suppose you don't have anything else you can offer your customers. You only have one product or service to sell.

What then?

Look around at complimentary, but non-competing businesses and see what products or services they might provide that you could offer to your customers. You want products or services that would be logical compliments to what you offer.

Then make arrangements with the businesses that provide those products to make them available to your customers. Remember, if your product and service really will help your customers solve their particular problems... if it really is in their best interest to purchase from you then...you have a moral obligation to see that they (your customer) get the very best use of that product or service.

And that may mean that you develop other products that will help them maximize the use of your product available to them... even if you don't sell them yourself.

Marketing Mistake #6 - Not Selling To Your Existing Customers

Your best prospects are people who have purchased from you before. They have already experienced the products you offer as well as the service you provide.

They know you, like you and trust you. At least they did when they first bought from you... enough, at least, to give you their money. Hopefully, things haven't changed. And ideally, your relationship with them has improved.

Research shows that it costs around five times more to acquire a new customer than it does to sell something additional to an existing customer.

So, if nothing else, it makes good financial sense to attempt to sell more to your existing customers before looking outside for new prospects.

One of the best ways for doing this is to constantly keep in touch with them. Make it impossible for them to forget you. Let them know you really appreciate not only their business, but their friendship, as well.

One of the best and most effective methods is to send a newsletter to your clients. You can publish articles of interest to them, and at the same time, let them know of special, "customer only" sales or special items they may be interested in at reduced prices.

If you have a "Referral Reward" program that rewards your customers for referring others to you, you can publish the results in your newsletter. This reminds your other customers about your program, and may entice them to participate in it.

Your newsletter can be published monthly, every two months or even quarterly. It really doesn't matter. The most important thing, is to keep in touch and get your name in front of them in a welcome, non-threatening way, on a regular, consistent, and predictable basis.

But remember, people don't necessarily care about what you care about, or your business. They care about what they care about.

So, make sure your newsletter contains items of interest to them.

Marketing Mistake #7 - Not Creating Joint Ventures

A great way to increase the odds that your marketing campaign will be a profitable success is to leverage the relationships other businesses have with their existing customers. By teaming up with another business you can create a win-win relationship for yourself and your teammate.

In the world of marketing, we call this 'teaming up' a Joint Venture. Joint Ventures can be one of the most profitable things you can do. And they usually turn out to be win-win situations.

Here's how an example Joint Venture might work:

A financial planner can arrange with an insurance agent to provide a complimentary 20-minute financial consultation with the agent's clients.

The insurance agent provides the list of names and writes a letter (paid for by the financial planner) to his or her clients making the complimentary offer as a "thank you" for doing business with the agent. The client gets the feeling that the agent cares about them, and gets a free 20-minute consultation from the financial planner.

They may even contract with the financial planner to do some additional work for them. The insurance agent gets to contact his clients in a non-threatening way essentially saying here's another service I provide for you and a thank you for being a client. The financial planner gets to show off his skills and expertise to someone they've never met (and may never have had the opportunity to meet), with the potential of gaining a new client.

In this situation, everyone wins…the insurance agent, the financial planner and the client. This same scenario can happen in any business.

Look around for businesses that provide complimentary, but non-competing services. See if you can arrange similar joint ventures with them. You can set up an arrangement where you get a percentage of the profits of any sales made to your clients. Or, you may choose to approach it as just another service you can provide your clients, and build more goodwill with them.

The opportunities are endless...and they really work!

Bonus Section #2

4 Powerful Strategies Guaranteed To Grow <u>Any</u> Business

Consistently being able to attract new customers must be a top goal for any business. However, there's more way to grow a business than just consistently attracting new customers.

I've included this Bonus Section dedicated to four methods that you can use to grow *any* business. These four methods are foundational building blocks that can be used by any business, in any industry, of any size.

4 Powerful Strategies Guaranteed To Grow Your Business

Growing a small business today can be very confusing. There's information and experts coming at you from every direction all pitching the "latest and greatest" sales or marketing technique. Some of these techniques work, and some are just there to create hype and sell books.

The good news is that there are fundamentals to growing a business that are universal for every industry. The three business growth fundamentals are:

1. Get more customers

2. Sell more to the customers you currently have

3. Get your customers to make more frequent purchases

Sure it's always easier said than done but once you break growing your business down to a fundamental level, you can focus all of your sales and marketing activities on what needs to be done.

Let's take a look at a few strategies that you can use to build your business on top of the fundamentals of business growth.

Step #1 Lead Generation

The best place to start is by looking at what activities you're currently using to generate leads for your product or service. To get a new customer you have to start with a lead.

Most small businesses tend to generate leads by using Yellow Pages ads (or other telephone directory advertising), the Internet and direct mail.

When it comes to generating leads, there are many methods to accomplish the task. Some methods are more cost effective than others. Some produce more qualified leads. Some will just never work for your target market.

I have identified over 80 methods for a small business to generate new leads. Of course you don't need to use all 80 to successfully generate qualified leads for your business.

You should start by looking at your current lead generating efforts and determine if your efforts are producing the number of leads you need to successfully grow your business. The statistics have proven that even a poor sales person will make a sale if he/she can get in front of enough people.

If you know that you need 100 leads to make one sale and you need to make 5 sales a day, then somehow you need to get your sales message in front of 500 people per day.

Step #2 Conversion Rate

Once you have a steady stream of leads coming in, it's then time to take a look at your conversation rate.

Conversion rate is simply the percentage of leads that become a customer. If you generate 100 leads per week from a specific campaign and 10 of those leads become a customer, then your conversion rate is 10%.

In order to accurately determine your conversion rate, you need to track the results of each of your marketing campaigns.

When I start working with new clients and I inquire about conversion rates, my clients often tell me they're converting at 80% to 90%. Conversion numbers like this are incredible and every marketer's dream.

But when I ask my client if I can see the actual data from the marketing campaign, they tell me they don't track any data. Then I know that their 80% conversion rate is fallacy. What that conversion rate is, is the business owner's or sales manager's wish i.e. what he actually wants his conversion rate to be.

To start measuring conversion rate, you need to track some metrics. These metrics include, cost of campaign, number of inquiries, number of inquiries that become customers, profit margin of product they bought, etc.

Once you start to actually measure your conversion rate, you can start to make changes in your sales and marketing efforts to increase that rate at which your leads are converting.

Step #3 Frequency of Purchase

One of the most difficult things for a business to do is to create a new customer. Getting someone to buy from you the first time is a very difficult task. Think about it, your customer needs to find you out of all the competition, you need to carry the specific item your customer is looking for, you need to be there when they're ready to buy and you needed to make it easy for them to make the purchase.

Then there's the one little factor called trust. About 80% of any purchase comes down to your customer trusting that what they are about to buy is going to work as promised.

Most small businesses make a crucial mistake when attempting to grow. The mistake is that they never capitalize on the trust that they built with their customer. Instead they forget about this trust and go out and generate more new leads to get new customers. In generating new leads, you have to start building trust all over again with someone new.

Businesses are so busy trying to get more leads that they neglect the fact that their current customers can be a great asset and great market for potential sales.

You see, by focusing on getting new customers, your business is really only doing "one shot" sales. You get a new customer, only sell to them one time, then you go and look for more new leads hoping to convert them to a customer.

How dramatic would your business change if instead of selling to each of your customers one time, you could get them to make two or three more additional purchases?

This strategy can be used in any business, from retail to healthcare. Once you get a new customer continue to follow-up with them and ask them if they are interested in buying from you again and again.

Step #4 Transaction Value

Here's a strategy that has been pioneered by many fast-food restaurants. It's just about impossible today to go into any fast-food restaurant and not have the cashier ask if you "want fries with that?" or "would you like to value size for only 30 cents more?"

Fast-food restaurants understand transaction value. They've realized that getting their customers to spend just a few more cents each time they make a purchase has a big impact on the day's sales figures.

Don't misunderstand me, I'm not advocating that you go out and "sell" every customer on buying more but there's nothing wrong with merely asking if they want to buy a complementary item when they make a purchase.

Notice I said complementary item with their purchase. If you're selling coffee, ask them if them want a muffin. If you're selling computers, do they need a mouse or software.

How can you increase the transaction size in your business?

Bonus Section #3

How to Quickly & Profitably Grow <u>Any</u> Business With Little or No Additional Money or Risk

Building a business can be a very expensive endeavor. Over time, your biggest expense is probably going to be the cost you incur to acquire customers. Depending on the size of your business, you can spend tens of thousands of dollars all the way to millions of dollars just to market your business with the hopes of building a solid customer base.

You'll not only incur an expense when marketing to generate prospects and new customers but to sustain longevity in the marketplace, you'll need to work diligently to build customer loyalty. Not to mention that when you advertise and market your business, you're also paying for the people who will never read any of your promotional material. How's that for waste?

You no longer have to waste your advertising and marketing budget on unqualified prospects and those who will never read your promotional material again. There's a shortcut that you can use to significantly increase the power of your marketing efforts and generate more in leads and customers in less time than ever before.

This shortcut is called a Joint Venture.

What is a Joint Venture?

Before I explain exactly what a Joint Venture is, let me explain a little about how people decide what products or services they're going to buy.

There are actually many reasons as to why people buy a specific product or service. They buy for enjoyment, efficiency, security and many other reasons.

Many people buy based on the trust that they have with someone. That someone might be an advisor, doctor or a loved one. If a person they trust makes a recommendation of your product of service, then the odds are in your favor that your prospect will buy.

With that said, wouldn't it make the most sense to find a "trusted advisor" to your prospective customers and work with the trusted advisor to bring your products to your prospects?

A Joint Venture (JV) is when two parties join together to share resources to accomplish a specific goal.

I most cases, one party has access to a specific market and has a distribution channel in place to reach this market. The second party usually brings with it a product or service that the market can benefit from that the first party can't provide.

In short, Party B has a product or service and Party A has customers that need or would benefit from the product of Party B.

How Use A Joint Venture To Grow Your Business

At the very beginning of this bonus section, I revealed that the biggest expense in your business is the cost of customer acquisition. Since you'll always need to acquire new customers, you'll never be able to avoid spending money to advertise and market your business.

You can't eliminate the cost associated with customer acquisition but you can lower it. By using a Joint Venture, you can slash your customer acquisition costs down to almost nothing, to almost zero.

You'll never be able to eliminate the cost totally because they'll always be some cost associated with getting new customers. It might be the cost of a mailing, the cost of man-hours to develop the promotion and then there's the cost associated with taking the order.

The most common form of a Joint Venture is called and endorsement. An endorsement is when Party A recommends and praises the product or service of Party B to his customers.

This endorsement can take the form of a letter, email or phone. The critical key to success is that Party A makes it clear that he is recommending, to his customers, what Party B has to offer.

As long as Party A has the trust of his customers, his customers will welcome the recommendation of Party B's product. Because this trust exists, you'll experience a lower barrier of resistance and Party A's customers will be more likely to buy your product.

Your business will grow when you take the cost savings from a lower cost acquisition cost and direct it toward activities that'll bring your greater profits, such as an investment in marketing or another capital expenditure. Plus, your JV agreement can be arranged in a manner so that if you agreed to pay the other party a commission for their help and access to their customers, you can pay any monies due out of the profit from the joint venture.

In addition, as long as you delivered on the product you offered and it meet the benefits you promised, you now have additional customers who know look to you as a "trusted advisor". Your trusted advisor status will lead to a higher customer lifetime value.

How to Setup a Joint Venture

Setting up a Joint Venture can be both easy and difficult. It can be as easy as a handshake and as difficult as big think legal agreements and a team of lawyers. When I'm looking to enter a Joint Venture partnership or alliance, I look for parties that lean toward a "gentlemen's handshake" with a simple agreement so we all understand our roles.

To setup a Joint Venture, first you want determine which businesses you should approach. Think about what kind of business would have customers that are very similar to your customers. Then determine what product or service can you can offer that would benefit their customers.

Next, simply contact the business. How you contact is up to you but your goal is to explain that you have a win-win proposition for them and explain the terms. Be sure to explain how the deal will work financially for both parties. Who will pay which costs and how will profits be divided.

Then simply get a signed agreement and execute your plan. Monitor the progress of the Joint Venture as time goes on and make any necessary changes to reap maximum profits from your alliance.

Keys to Success in a Joint Venture

As with most things in life that are specific keys that when followed will almost guarantee success. Here are a few keys that will contribute to your success in Joint Ventures.

1. Set clear goals. Seems kind of obvious but goals are often overlooked. Not only should you think about your goals but also the goals of your Joint Venture partner.

2. Take your time. Business happens fast and you want to be able to quickly adapt to changes in your marketplace. When it

comes to Joint Ventures, my recommendation is to take your time. Take your time when searching for the appropriate JV partner. You want to take your time and find someone you can trust and work with on an ongoing basis.

3. Look to the future. I've found that while the majority of the people in the world are honest, some are not. You want to prepare and guard yourself from any future legal challenges that may or may not arise. Make sure everything is in writing and you and your JV partner fully understand the terms and agreement.

4. Nurture the JV relationship. Once you've determined that your JV partnership is working, take time to build trust and understanding with your partner. By communicating details about your JV campaigns' performance and your future JV goals, you'll start to build an ongoing alliance.

Examples of Joint Ventures

The types of Joint Ventures you could setup are endless. Here are just a few samples of some very basic Joint Venture arrangements.

1. Scott is the owner of a fitness center. Scott's sales have been stagnant and his marketing efforts are performing poorly. Scott approaches the local radio station and offers free memberships to the morning radio crew and DJ if, once a day, they mention on the air how much they enjoy working out at Scott's fitness center.

2. Hillary is a dentist who owns his own practice and has been having trouble getting new patients. Hillary knows how important healthy teeth are to a good smile and a good smile is part of looking beautiful. Hillary approaches her hair stylist, Jane, and she and Jane develop a package called "Hair, Health & Beauty". Who someone purchases this package, they get a hair cut and style along with a teeth whitening procedure all for one price.

Both Hillary and Jane market this package to their clients. Now some of Hillary's patients become clients of Jane and vice-versa.

3. Tommy owns a local Quick Lube oil changing station. He approaches a few of the car dealership in the area and offers to give all new car purchasers a coupon for a free oil change. Tommy supplies the coupons and all the car dealerships have to do is give them away as a bonus for buying a new car. The dealerships get to give to give each buyer a free gift for their purchase and Tommy gets a steady stream of customers.

Summary

Using Joint Ventures in your marketing efforts can be a very effective manner for acquiring new customers and reducing your marketing costs. A JV also will eliminate some of the apprehensiveness of your prospect. Since your prospect's trusted advisor is recommending your product or service, they're more inclined to make a purchase from you.

Closing Remarks

Many business owners complain about not having enough new customers. What most don't realize is that they are actually bringing it upon themselves.

It has nothing to with the economy, changes to tax laws, or how well the stock market is doing. Disgruntled business owners tend to blame their failure on everything under the sun. Very few accept responsibility for their own results.

Even of those who do accept responsibility for their results, very few of them will actually get off their butt and do something about it. Everyone wants more customers, more sales and more profits, but very few want to do the work to get more.

To reach your goals, whether in business or life, you've got to take action. You can't sit back and do nothing. To start attracting new customers, use the strategies in this book combined with Massive Action.

To your success,
Michael John Alos
www.MichaelAlos.com

How To Get More Information From The Author

Michael Alos is a marketing consultant, speaker and direct-response copywriter. He works primarily with small-business owners, speakers, consultants, and coaches who want to create direct response mail, advertising and Internet marketing campaigns to boost revenue and generate qualified leads for their businesses.

To learn more about Michael consulting services or for information about having Michael speak at your association or company's convention or meetings, or to view a catalog of his other books and audio courses, visit his website at:

www.MichaelAlos.com

Bonus Gifts

As a purchaser of this book, you are entitled to free bonus gifts that will supplement what you've read in this book and help you in implementing these strategies in your business.

Grab your free bonus gifts valued at $47 by visiting:

www.CustomerAttractionBook.com/free